Optimal Avenues p1

Awakenings

To Ʒ̶Ꝑ̶ Charlotte
With Best Wishes
Gwen McNamara
ph: 07891427536

poetry by

Gwen McNamara

MOTHWING PRESS

Mothwing Press
mothwingpress@mothwing.com

or contact Gwen McNamara at:
optimalavenues@eircom.net

Photography by Terry Milligan,
Gwen McNamara, Valerie Lawson,
Steve Levesque & Andy Levesque
Paintings ©2002 by Veronica Heywood
"Legendary Landscape Collection"
and Ukrainian painter Mikura (p45)

Cover image and book design
by Andy Levesque

Printed in the United States
Second Edition

ISBN 0-9724528-1-8

Acknowledgements

Warm thanks to Veronica Heywood, whose paintings accompany my poetry and to Andy Levesque and his brother Steve, who took my futuristic vision in their hands and made this collection possible.

In appreciation to the "Culture of Peace organisation and to the kind people on both sides of the Atlantic Ocean who have helped me turn dreams into reality.

This work is dedicated to my family. My mother Bridie and children: Clodagh, Yvonne, Simon, Tirzah, grandsons Brian and John, and for my late father - Jim. Finally to my Leitrim friend and poet Mary Guckian, for her continues support of all my endeavours.

This work is also dedicated to the Nameless who suffer and die from human rights violations. May the Culture of Peace Collaborative make a difference?

Contents

perfect harmony
weaving rustic mosaic
the chipmunk and I

ONE UN-LIT MORNING IN HOWTH

It fell from azure blurred
One Un-lit Morning,
Seeking the incomplete.
Shone a luminous spectrum
On autumn's dusty shade.
Carpet foliage yawned
Tilting towards light
Where whispered breezes formed.
Spring became
A pressie of enchantment
Mystical crescendo
Budding cloud.
Awakening narcissus seed
Sung the sanctioned sonnet
Resounding through trees.
Chrysanthemums sprayed the forest,
Scarlet, purple, white.
Arrayed with green,
One Un-lit Morning,
Stilled the Owl-eyed night.

LIFE ITSELF

Out of the Ashes
Gilded smouldering sky.
Stench flesh perfumes
Another plundered village
This Holy Death

From your Benediction Urn
Innocence spiral upwards.
Fragrance from your fragrance
Created this
Paradoxical pageantry.

Balancing precariously unbridled life
Tucked within unopened wombs.
You have come to salvage what is lost.
Guarding only in your safe-keeping
Life itself.

BETWEEN DUBLIN AND LEITRIM

In Loving Memory of My Uncle Tom

I was misplaced
In the Metropolis,
Between city and country,
Dublin and Leitrim.
Where sodden turf
Sweetened over crackling fire.
We washed in rain barrel water
And picked hen soiled eggs
Rode Donkeys backwards
While going on mystery tours
Across the farm.

We lifted bales of hay
When sun bent on tanning bodies
Sweated our effort.
Surrendering to
Thick batch ham slices
With stewed tea
I remember you - Uncle Tom
My second father,
Clay pipe, tobacco essence,
That "hoar of a fence"
You constantly repaired.

Mid afternoon studying
The "fat lady"
Drinking beer in Mohil
You drew that pipe,
As sucking grass sheaves,
"I could keep her for a week,
But I couldn't feed her
For a day"
You finally mused,
Wandering through
The garden of youth.

Years later I took that path
To the house of over 200 years,
I stood at your coffin
To say "goodbye"
Adorned in your 50th Wedding
Anniversary Suit, I remembered
With pride, your term
As Leitrim's Lord-Mayor
Tears spilt into joined hands
I kissed your cheeks
Harder still to let go.

perched on birdhouse branch
sensing my intrusion
tree swallows flee

oileán
na
móan
uaisle-

THE VOYAGE OF BRAN

A woman from unknown lands
Sang on the floor of the house
To Bran the son Of Febal:

Landscaped on
An evening's sun
In misty shade she hides
Magical tingling masts
Beckon Him to the Harbour side

As ancient tree
There is with blossoms
On which birds
Call the hours

I will dance and romance
To your chants,
My magical mystical seer
Queen of Maids from Ladies Isle
Beckons you to Brandon Pier

Come hither on land
O Bran Son of Febal
Welcome is thy advent
To Ladies Isle

Will Bran fear
The echoed shrill
Like a Gannet call
From the harbour wall
Her drawing near

Honeysuckle cascading
Over Brandon Pier
Perfumes its entrance
Land of Youth-Tir Na Oige

I'll bathe with you
In misty shade
Imprint on the Night
Like a vessel seeding moist
Eternally lost in flight

SAOIRSE

Beyond the firmament
clothed by waves,
Neptune's Myriad Nymphs
swim from his sunken bed
of slimy shoal.
Tucked within this leafy shade
silence spawns silver netting
over their absence.

Saoirse his narcissus seed
Weaves aesthetic sheen
Across the oceans edge.
Magical Mystical Being,
Radiant countenance
Beckoned those that hide.
Neptune's myriad nymphs
To her side.

CREAKING HOUSE

Lulled in lullaby
Creaking house settles
Crackling turf's bogged scent
Perfumes this archive.
Quaint silent aftermath
Mounted on white-washed walls
Woodcutter's carvings
Create their own identity

Life-span continuity,
Horse harness, brass measures,
Billycans, bellows, leaded kettles
Mingle with freshly painted masks.
Creative skilled hands
Mounting new expression
For the Sligo Summer festival

What crooked fingers lit
Gas lanterns on winter evenings,
What breath blew winded instruments
Melodious as the fiddlers dance
On concrete parlour floor
What hands built
Rugged bedroom walls,
Indelible childish laughter
Sealing each stone.

Where lamentations glisten
Rain upon barren mountains,
Desolate twilight claimed
One of your own.
Seeing the Coronation
Of her Majesty
Queen Elizabeth The Second
Emigration-did it steal the rest?

leaning wild ferns
approaching winter's bleak
emerald fusion

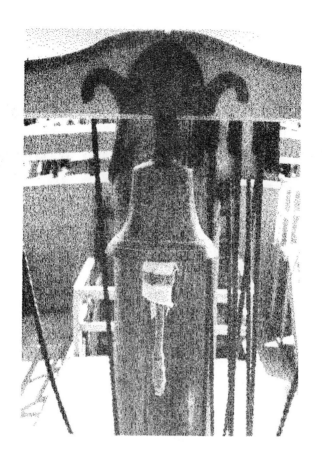

SANDS OF TIME

Compatible comely silence,
Tock ticks tedious hours
This legendary decade.
The hourglass
Spilling memoirs
Stormy shifting sands
Through Nocturnal dreams
Sometimes-even now
Harmonize his sleep.

Remembering other Cities,
Distant shores.
Seagulls squeaking over spoil.
Neon lights illuminating tide.
The salty taste
Of misted air.
Dry eyes splashed
By spurting waves,
Strong hands scrubbing decks

Exiled to solitary rooms
Called house or home
Clicking cutlery for one.
Moist fingers groping
Hardened clay,
Planting daffodils
This wintering year,
He remembers spring
Budding through hibernation.

Sometimes-even now,
His equilibrium sways,
Like planted tulips
In morning's air.
He sips tea listening.
He's always listening
To the tick tock,
Chiming fruitless tomorrow's
Ills endless days.

ETERNALLY STRONG

Sometimes at mid-day
She dreams colour.
And in the dead of night
When mosquitoes hum
And crickets crawl
She meanders
Through a labyrinth
Off webbed waves
Flowing onwards,
Upward, towards sky.
Bobbing in the houseboat
Off formative years,
Where luminous shadows
Even then,
Cast Payne shades.

Sometimes during day
She sips merlot
Where words create
New images on
Yielding pages.
Depth falls, falls
From spoken lips.
The in-between world
Filters through,
Darkness and light,
She is a survivor,
Free flowing Spirit
Eternally strong,
A sojourner on
Earthly planes.

NIGHT TREMORS

Cries the hunted
Cry of wolves,
Shrill and piercing
In the night,
Echoed by spent shells
NATO explosions.
Atrocities to end
All atrocities,
To halt the internal struggle,
Scavengers in a land
That was never theirs to inhabit.

You made sure they knew
Their place,
Your legacy carnage,
Villages on the run,
Even the selection process
Under sixteen – over sixty
Men separated stand in line
Their surety death,
Silently they move
In single file
At your command.

Slit throats, broken bodies
Albanian refugees,
Nights that shelter terror,
Perhaps genocide began
The day or night your parents
Individually committed suicide.
Slobodan Milosevic,
You craved to fill the void,
Plague that delivers
The depraved
Onto self-destruction.

Where masses followed
A voice in their wilderness,
The piper piped and Serbs danced
You were their tune.
Layer upon layer unfolding,
Within the smouldering recess
Off tormented minds,
Huddled in thousands.
They cannot comprehend.
How nights became eternity
And eternity became their nights.

under the shadows
brighter than the sun-lit grass
the spring splashes green

MIDNIGHT'S CLOAK

Ebony shelters distant waves
Woven tranquil balm
Forever stilled.
No preying seagull wing
To dive on spoil,
No murmuring ship
Moving gently to shore.
No beacon to guide,
Eerie shadowed angles
With phantom feelers
Luring curious eyes
Peeping shyly,
Where agape sockets
Surrender tendrils,
Forever coyly stare.

Ode to spent scenario,
Where crescendo waves
Spew phantom formations.
Rocks surface
As ghostly sea lions
Sipping ebony cup
Where orb shimmers
Neon sheen
Where sleeping waves
Yawn and stretch
Across the waters edge
In this stilled hour
Clothed with ebony
The moon is lost to view
Tucked in Midnight's Cloak.

DESECRATION

Encased in rigor mortis
the brown shrouded shell
lay on its dipped bed
I saw first its mirrored reflection
tasting the crisp smell
where waxing candles
paid homage
like painted angels
on deserted cathedral walls.
I drew near
to him the departed
to the "him" we called "Pops"
memories rested on the silent one
which graced my presence,
A kindred Spirit

and I was cautioned
to revere that which lay dead
and kiss the marble mouth,
the protruding lips
where iced air
blew phantom breath.
I drew near,
"Pops" I whispered
and shivered fear.
I could almost hear him say,
"Well, be the hokey, you
bate me at draughts"
And I knew he'd allowed me to.
I caressed
the silver sheaves
that stood edged
on the silent one's forehead,
and plucked the tuft,
offering a curled posy
to a cousin
who should warm his memory.
I became the protagonist
on an eclipsed stage.
condemned for desecrating.
They buried my innocence
the day they buried him.

moss woven rock
against the dark canyon mouth
reaping dusty gold

Dedicated to those who died by Atomic Warfare
in Hiroshima. August 6th 1945

MUST BE ONE OF OURS

Under wings the silver shaft
Eased forward.
Cyanide capsules on the reserve
(Just in case)
They retained their eclipse shade
Over a quickened City
Where nerved sinews frayed.
Hiroshima stood still
Beneath the facade
Of charcoal fires burning
Heating what remained
He ate - perturbed
By words which spoke
Both victory and death.

Two opposing forces
Like one unbalanced equation
His numbed senses - stirred.

Shaking like a dog
Without its master
He shuffled down the street
Where children played.
Barefooted in the dusty heat
He reached the Osaka Bank.

And in his vague awareness
A B29 hovered overhead
'Must be one of ours'
he confidently said.

He was translated
By the translucent ray
(Which must be one of ours)
Imprinted on the concrete slabs,
Undone, he raveled
Just like an unthreaded rag doll.

His contour echoed
The anguished cry
Where screams from scorched skins
And particles of incinerated flesh
Bloated the Ohta River

A City Dead

And moving shrouded phantoms
With parched lips
Which vomited red
With every breath
That breathed words
Which sounded like
Peace, peace, peace

November 6th 03 and Beyond
For Dad

Death is but Breath
A Hesitant Release
From Earth Boundaries

Beyond Limitation
The Spirit Rises
Vacating this Form

Abundant knowledge
Wisdom and insight
Are Yours

Deeper Your Presence
Listening, Lingering Soul
Peaceful Journey Home

BOSTON TAKE-OFF
TWILIGHT IN MASSACHUSETTS ~ LOGAN AIRPORT ~ 18.8.00

The plane moves slowly towards takeoff.
Wheels crunch gnawing gravel
While I watch boats glide
On Boston Harbour,
Landscaped rustic edgings
Approaching autumn's Harvest.

I will to write

To come to terms with departure,
To glimpse last minute delight,
Boston glittering.
I visualize City Hall,
Boston Common - North End
Window seat at wing.

Soon I'll glide like a bird

Facing North - figuratively speaking
I'll even get to see Maine.
Thundering forward on racetrack
City lights twinkle- descend
Fuel flashes lightning in air
Flying over ocean.

Butterflies in tummy

Twilight surrenders to darkness
As we climb beyond visibility.
Beyond the firmament of familiar
Skyline sweeps westward,
Launching sunset-red shift
Stretching, bronze & turquoise, green,

Across an Indigo Sky

Cruising through the ordained
Ordinance between - time and space.
Tumbling into Sunset over and over,
Undiscovered Seashore.
Ebony flakes obscure vision momentary.
I am lost to describe

The Splendour of this new discovery.

39

Poll Dubh
Burron, Co. Clare

Hesitant footing
Spewing mud platter
Plunged posteriors,
Into sucked depth
Crawling we mingled
With mire
And climbed void.
The torched beam
Our only beacon,
As water sogged footing
Seeking security
Searched the contoured bleakness.

While our hosts,
In jagged formation
Ritually celebrate
The carboniferous age,
Where calcium stalactites
Dripped icicles
Tempting touch,
Arrayed with rugged detachment
Toffee stained, glistening.

Hands traced indented coral
Carved in Mudpack rock.
A gushing cascade
Lamented
The mundane wading
From water clogged Wellingtons.
This Archaeologist Lair,
Indelible Artefact,
Poll Dubh, the dark hole
darker still.

ONLY JUSTICE

Dedicated to Edward O'Neill
Victim of Dublin's Bombings
May 17th ~ 26 died & 253 injured.

Poised amidst innocence lost
You bear your predators no evil.
Pawns in the hands of a higher intellect
Dublin and Monaghan's dead
Cry for recognition.
Severed, misplaced each face scarred and stilled.
While anguish echoed as thunderous
Waves thrashing barren shores
Silently sands shelved the nullified.
Jigsaw remnants incomplete
Where justice remained beyond the grasp
Of even law itself.

And you, just five, caught
Between a nation's conflict
Yawning yarns played centuries before birth.
On the morning of another's evening
You would cease to chase magical childhood charms.
Security spilt like an egg timer
For dissolving grain was your face.
You lay, huddled on the pavement
The dead man beside you was Da.
You soared beyond revenge
To an honourable noble place,
Courageously seeking justice.

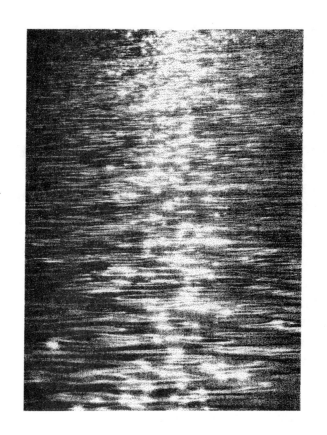

moon clothed with clouds
suddenly sheds each layer
sea sparkles and shines

REMEMBRANCE DAY
NOVEMBER 1987
The Enniskillen Bombings

Bomb which severed
Body from soul
Dropped
Onto Remembrance Day
Showered their silent salute
As they remembered their dead
Like dew drops
On moistened clay
They poured
Into the assailant's chalice
And while they danced
Their jubilant dance
The earth drank
Victims cooling blood
On Remembrance Day
Where eleven who remembered
Surrendered to clay.

RADICAL AVENUES

This delible crucible
Overflowed with isolation
As I walked
Through st. Michael's fields.
Though cherry-blossom trees bloomed,
Though daffodils and tulips
Intoxicated the spring air
They beckoned me to dwell
In their haven
Here I walked In self-communion,
Seeking Solace
Amid the comeliness.

I remembered the bullocks
I once stroked
The smoky dung, slimy, infested
And the crawling navy blue. Oh how
That nauseous steam mingled
With the Summer breeze.
At the distant partitioned fence
Cattle sagged, grunting.
With outstretched hands
I offered them rushes,
They remained astute,
And, brown eyed, they eyed me.
Suck, suck, suck.

At this graveyard I once stalled
In its stillness, the upturned sods
Awaited their destined cortege.
In its stillness I remembered
God my Saviour, the Alpha
And the Omega

I recall the chuckles from
My children
As they tumbled
Down the slopes to land
Smack, on the gravel path.
"Mama can kiss"
all thing better, better;
Adventures around the grotto,
Playing hide and seek,

Becoming Robin Hood for
Just one hour,
Climbing the creeping ivy
To reign-all Kings.

I remember Autumn's acorns
Underneath the amber leaves
Prickling my youngsters' hands.
Impish faces glowed
As they stripped them
to shining brown,
Then secured
To bulging pockets

Then conveniently dumped
On teacher's nature table,
Then Tomorrow,
Always, the assurance of a tomorrow,
All-innocent and beautiful.

Clasping fantasy with understanding
Where reality and imagination are
But fraternal twins fashioned
Through their corded childhood.

Allow them the privilege to be
Freed from human cages
Time will teach these factors
Oh too soon.
Do not waive their gentle musing.
Do not heedlessly
Dish out plates of pain
Borne through the frustration
Of one's own inadequacy.

The I that must
Always appear in control
Lest the I that must,
Should lose direction.

As for me, I dwell upon
Precarious, disjointed reflections,
A lonely place to inhabit.
Deep within the shredded core
Lives a loner
Alone when it matters.
I am a recluse,
A facet for all
The countless people
I have encountered.
Yet I still choose
The fated maze chambers
Chiselled by me - for me

Though the fragrant roses serenade,
And though their thorns may penetrate
Beyond human endurance,
This is breath.
This is blood,
This is life,
And the rational decision
May not always be
The all in all.
You will find me,
If you care to find me,
Drifting through these
Radical avenues, always - always

the opened window
butterfly on angel wings
flowers in my hand

peace
is in
our hands

Celebrating MANIFESTO 2000 (UNESCO)
for a culture of peace and non-violence

The year 2000 must be a new beginning for us all. Together we can transform the culture of war and violence into a culture of peace and non-violence. This demands the participation of everyone. It gives young people and future generations values that can inspire them to shape a world of dignity and harmony, a world of justice, solidarity, liberty and prosperity. The culture of peace makes possible sustainable development, protection of the environment and the personal fulfillment of each human being.

Recognizing our share of responsibility for the future of humanity, especially for today's children and those of future generations, we choose to respect the life and dignity of every person without discrimination or prejudice, defend freedom of expression and cultural diversity, giving preference always to dialogue and listening, rather than fanaticism, defamation and the rejection of others.

We also choose to practice non-violence in all its forms: physical, sexual, psychological, and social, in particular towards the most deprived and vulnerable, such as children and adolescents, and to devote our energies to put an end to exclusion, injustice and political and economic and oppression.

Together we pledge to promote consumer behavior that is responsible and development practices that respect all forms of life and help preserve the balance of nature on the planet.

Gwen McNamara is a freelance writer and a member of the Irish National Union of Journalists. She is on the Editorial panel of the "Concrete News" and is the founder and coordinator of the mixed media productions, Mirrored Days - Un-Mirrored Nights and the ongoing Optimal Avenues Annual Festival.

Gwen has been writing since childhood. Her published works include "Between the Circus and Sewer" and "Rainbows and Stone," in *Poetry Plus Anthology 1993/94*, "Is Anyone Listening," in *Spring Poets 1974* and in *Journal of Modern Writing*, Boston 2001. This is her first Anthology, a compilation of older and more recent works, some in haiku format. Gwen's poetry has been featured in performance both in Massachusetts and Ireland. She draws inspiration from nature, the people and traditions of Ireland, and from the world's yearning for peace and justice. An online gallery of her poetry can be found at www.mothwing.com/galleries/gwenmcnamra

Her poetry has played an important part in the "Culture of Peace" Exhibit, a cross-cultural collaboration of writers and visual artists fusing their work to celebrate the United Nations Mandate for Peace. Gwen was instrumental in bringing this group together. The exhibit – compelling and eclectic, has been displayed in a number of New England art galleries, with more planned, its theme clearly significant for our times.